CLASSIC NARROW BOATS

MALCOLM RANIERI

HALSGROVE

First published in Great Britain in 2013

Copyright © Malcolm Ranieri 2013

All rights reserved. No part of this publication may be reproduced, stored in a retrieval system, or transmitted in any form or by any means without the prior permission of the copyright holder.

British Library Cataloguing-in-Publication Data
A CIP record for this title is available from the British Library

ISBN 978 0 85704 204 0

HALSGROVE
Halsgrove House,
Ryelands Business Park,
Bagley Road, Wellington, Somerset TA21 9PZ
Tel: 01823 653777   Fax: 01823 216796
email: sales@halsgrove.com

Part of the Halsgrove group of companies.
Information on all Halsgrove titles is available at: www.halsgrove.com

Printed in China by Everbest Printing Co Ltd

INTRODUCTION

Today, road transport is the major mover of goods and raw materials. Previous to that the railways from the mid-Victorian period held sway, and of course, some bulk freight is still carried that way. It is difficult to imagine now that before that in the 1800s and lingering into the mid-1900s though very much reduced, the canals and navigable rivers of Britain were the major transport network. Nowadays the canals are an expanding leisure industry, and hardly any cargo is carried. Enthusiasts have restored canals and working narrow boats as living history over the last sixty years or so, after the transport of goods and raw materials had all but disappeared and the waterways themselves had been abandoned and in many cases become derelict.

Prior to the mid-eighteenth century transport of people and goods was slow and unreliable. It was mainly reliant on horse-power, and water-borne where navigable rivers existed (the Thames and Severn are examples), and coastal sea borne traffic. Away from the coast and navigable rivers, the roads apart from in some cities and towns were of a very low standard, and basically unsurfaced lanes, roughly surfaced with broken rocks or even just beaten earth, and rutted by the passing of carts: in winter frozen and in summer very often dusty. Some toll and parish roads were better maintained but overall the standard of roads on which goods and people were moved was poor, only improving substantially during the late-Victorian period. This situation caused a rethink on transport, due in the main to the onset of the so-called Industrial Revolution which occurred from around 1760 to the early-Victorian period. New methods of manufacture and supply of raw materials meant that transport had to keep pace, and artificial waterways was one form of transport which was seen to be a good part of the answer.

The artificial waterways or canals were built by famous canal engineers such as Thomas Telford, who built the Birmingham and Liverpool Junction Canal and Pontysyllte Viaduct on the Llangollen Canal; James Brindley who constructed many of the Midlands canals; John Rennie; John Smeaton; and Smeaton's understudy William Jessop who with Telford constructed the Caledonian Canal. Jessop also was Chief Engineer and with James Barnes built the Grand Junction Canal, which was to become the Grand Union. There were many thousands of labouring navvies who often by hand shifted millions of tons of earth to make the canal 'cut', and shaped the embankments, built the aqueducts and bridges, and constructed the tunnels, from 1760 to 1840 building this at the time revolutionary transport artery. This new form of transport allowed goods and raw materials to be transported from and to the industrial heartlands of this country via canals and rivers to ports and then to the rest of the world. At its zenith the inland waterway network stretched over 5000 miles and carried 30 million tonnes of goods and raw materials each year. The network linked raw materials' suppliers like mines and quarries with manufacturing centres, and the main towns, cities and harbours as never before allowing the Industrial Revolution to prosper.

The canals were owned and operated by private canal companies, such as the Grand Union Canal Carrying Company, Fellows, Morton & Clayton and the Birmingham Canal Navigation. With the canals in decline, and in the majority owned by the railways, when the railways were nationalised in 1948 they were transferred to the new British Transport Commission. Then in 1962 the Transport Act split railways from the canals. They became part of the British Waterways Board which controlled approximately 2000 miles of canals, and was sponsored by the Department for Environment (DEFRA) in England and Wales, and the Scottish Government in Scotland. The Transport Act, 1968 classified the nationalised waterways into three categories: commercial traffic (what little remained); cruising-leisure use; and the remainder for which no use could be seen. The canals in the remainder category therefore came to be abandoned very often, sinking into disrepair. On 2 July, 2012, British Waterways' assets and responsibilities were transferred to the charity the Canal and River Trust, in Scotland controlled by Scottish Canals. Often the rise of interest in canals is attributed to the author LTC (Tom) Rolt whose book *Narrow Boat* was published in 1944, Robert Aikman and Charles Hadfield, but a key development was the establishment of the Inland Waterways Association in 1946, which promoted use and restoration of the canals, and at the time the setting-up of boat-hire companies. British Waterways also operated from the late-1950s a holiday hire boat fleet. All this combined to open up the leisure side of canals and encourage volunteers, sometimes supported by local authorities, to restore the derelict, though often officially open, waterways a movement which still continues to this day.

In the early days of artificial waterways or canals in the late-eighteenth century and early nineteenth-century, because of cost, labour and geographic constraints, when constructed size was dictated by practicalities and economics. Therefore the vessels carrying goods and raw materials on the waterways were constructed according to the depth of water and dimensions of the locks. Locks are simply a device for transporting water-borne craft from one water level to another where gradients are encountered. The early canals were so built that the boats using them were generally ten times as long as they were wide, and with a loaded draught of three feet of water, hence the term narrow boat. The British narrow boat is up to 72 feet (21.95 metres) long and 7 feet (2.13 metres) wide, because of the limiting factor of the size of the locks. There are some exceptions to this in the United Kingdom: the Manchester Ship Canal in England and the Caledonian Canal in Scotland are examples where much bigger boats can be used. The technology of the day dictated that for the first one hundred years or so the narrow boats were of wood construction and pulled by horses. With the enormous advances in technology during the Victorian period, iron and steel boats were built, some steam driven and eventually the internal combustion engine took over. There was no clear cut changeover, and horse-pulled boats were still being built and in use up to the 1940s.

Narrow boats very often worked in pairs, though this in the main coincided with the use of the internal combustion engine in the narrow boats, with a 'butty' being towed behind the powered boat, the butty being an unpowered trailer boat to carry additional cargo. A 'joey' boat is typical of the Midlands and in particular the Birmingham Canal Navigation (BCN); these were open cargo boats, in use on the extensive but in distance short-haul systems in Birmingham and the Black Country. Built without cabs, occasionally with shelters, and not designed to be lived on, the joeys were originally of wood and then iron or steel construction, some double-ended with transferrable rudders or helms. Joeys were pulled by horses in the main, but were from time to time marshalled as 'trains' and pulled by powered tugs. The Midlands canals benefitted from this type of haulage and especially where cargo could be transferred to the railways, and generally the canal systems and boats were well maintained, as was not the case in other parts of the country.

The life of a canal boatman was hard, long days because of deadlines, and mostly poorly paid. Whilst the popular image is of the boatman's family living on board the boat as it worked the canals, this was not the case in the early days. It was in the 1830s that families started to accompany the owner/captain living in the cabin of the boat, mainly to work the boat harder, a ready crew, and to avoid rent, but also to keep the family together. Space in the cabin was restricted, but heated by a warm stove, and the decorations of brass, lace, painted housewares and decorated china made up a little for the cosy accomodation. However, it was difficult for the children to obtain an education always being on the move. The narrow boats have for many years been decorated with images of roses and castles and also the fixtures and fittings, the doors of the cabin, water cans etc and the side panels advertised in ornate lettering the boat's owner and name. Each carrying company would also have a distinctive livery. This was not universal however, and some canals and owners did not follow this practice, though the growth of leisure boating has seen this type of decoration proliferate.

As trade dropped off and in some areas disappeared after the Second World War, many systems became derelict, and some still are in that state. From the 1950s the preservation movement commenced and all over the country canals are being restored, very often by hard working volunteers, under the overall control of British Waterways. Those restored have seen major growth of ownership of narrow boats and tourism. Similarly, as the canal carrying of cargo virtually disappeared, the working narrow boats were very often discarded and became derelict like the canals, occasionally sunk after use, some converted to pleasure or trip boat use, cabins covering up bays where once coal or other raw materials were carried. A few carried on with specialist carriers, and British Waterways used some for maintenance on the existing network. Luckily like all our heritage in this country, there are some individuals or groups who want to own and preserve the past – in this case the historic working narrow boat. As the movement has gathered pace, boats in all conditions have been restored, some even raised from the water, and other boats converted as pleasure and hire boats have been re-converted to their working state, even a few faithful replicas have been constructed. There are still a handful of carriers working the canals, gatherings of working boats take place throughout the summer and there are active museums dotted around the canal systems, ensuring that the legacy of two hundred years of moving cargo on our artificial waterways is not forgotten.

In this book I have tried to illustrate the current preservation movement, with images of original boats, tugs and butties and joeys, replicas, steam boats, and others, mostly restored to original working condition by their enthusiastic owners, but also a few conversions to show all sides of the movement. There are a few images of the canal infrastructure, where not illustrated with the working boats. The majority of the images have been taken around the inland waterways of the Midlands where I live and where they were and still are used as they were intended for transport, though mostly now they are pleasure craft rather than carrying coal! It has been said many times, but worth repeating that "Birmingham and the Black Country has more canals than Venice", and I hope that this book will interest all that read it to go and have a look at their nearest canal, walk the towpaths, enjoy the scenery both urban and rural and the wildlife, marvel at the engineering, watch the boats go by and see how much they are enjoyed. I dedicate this book to those hard working volunteers who have and are currently restoring our canal network, and the preservationists who own, restore and display the historic working canal narrow boat. Long may this continue at four miles an hour, the speed limit on the majority of the inland waterways!

CANALS ON WHICH THE IMAGES WERE TAKEN AND MUSEUMS

Ashby Canal
Birmingham Canal Navigation – Main Line Canal
Coventry Canal
Droitwich Barge Canal
Dudley Canal
Grand Union Canal
Oxford Canal
Stratford upon Avon Canal
Trent and Mersey Canal
Worcester and Birmingham Canal

WATERWAYS MUSEUMS

Gloucester Waterways Museum, Llanthony Warehouse, Gloucester Docks, Gloucester GL1 2EH

The Canal Museum, Stoke Bruerne, Towcester, Northants NN12 7SE

Foxton Canal Museum, Middle Lock, Gumley Road, Foxton, Market Harborough, Leics LE16 7RT

Black Country Living Museum, Tipton Road, Dudley, West Midlands DY1 4SQ

National Waterways Museum, Ellesmere Port, Cheshire, L65 4FW

Kennet and Avon Canal Museum, Devizes Wharf, Couch Lane, Devizes, Wiltshire SN10 1EB

Basingstoke Canal Centre, Mytchett Place Road, Mytchett, Surrey GU16 6DD

Water Folk Museum, Old Store House, Llanfrynach, Brecon, Powys LD3 7LJ

Yorkshire Waterways Museum, Dutch River Side, Goole, East Yorkshire DN14 5TB

Union Canal Museum, Manse Road, Canal Basin, Linlithgow, West Lothian, Scotland

Fourteen Locks Canal Centre, Cwm Lane, Rogerstone, Gwent, Wales

Banbury Canal Museum, Spiceball Park Road, Banbury, Oxfordshire, OX16 2PQ

At 6.30am on 9 July, 2010, at Soulbury Three Locks, near Leighton Buzzard, five historic working narrow boats, one a replica, and a butty and a joey are ready to take part in the first leg of their journey up the Grand Union Canal from Paddington Basin to Atherstone. This is the loaded Gravel Run from London to the Midlands, a distance of 120 miles. At Paddington Basin contractors building the Terry Farrell building against the historic basin wall of 1801, had tipped 100 tons of gravel as reinforcement. The only means of removal of the gravel was via the Grand Union Canal, and a group of owners tendered and won the transportation contract, taking place from 5 to 11 July, 2010, using the Grand Union to Braunston, then to Hawkesbury Junction on the Oxford Canal, and finally the Coventry Canal to Atherstone where the gravel was unloaded. It was good to see the canals being used as they were intended, worthwhile economic and ecologically sound transport corridors, if maybe a little slow for today's deadlines.

Later on 9 July, 2010, at Willowbridge Marina, Bridge 99, on the Grand Union Canal *Themis* works north singly towards Milton Keynes. She is a Grand Union Canal Carrying Company Ltd (GUCC) motor boat of the Star class, fleet number 90, built in 1935 by Harland & Wolff, at Woolwich, London, with iron composite hull, a working boat now in the hands of Star Class Carrying Company, recently re-converted back to its original working boat state.

Also at Willowbridge Marina, Bridge 99, on 9 July, 2010, are working boat *Archimedes* and butty (GUCC unpowered boat) *Ara* both heavily loaded heading north on the Grand Union Canal towards Milton Keynes. It is thought that 'butty' is a corruption of the word 'buddy', or friend. *Archimedes* is a GUCC motor boat of the Star class, fleet number 12, built in 1935 by Harland & Wolff, at Woolwich, London, with steel composite hull. The boat was sold to Watneys Brewery from the GUCC, and converted to a trip boat called *Barleycorn*, now restored to original condition with an extended cabin.

Another working boat *Arundel* with in this case a joey (Birmingham Canal Navigation [BCN] terminology for an unpowered trailer boat) named *Joe* in tow, is seen at Willowbridge Marina, Bridge 99, on the Grand Union Canal on 9 July, 2010, both loaded with gravel proceeding north. *Arundel* is a faithful replica working boat, built in 2003, based on a GUCC motor Star class; the joey is an original boat.

The joey, named *Joe*, BCN day boat number 108, about to pass under a roadbridge, and heading north low in the water, loaded with gravel.

The Gravel Run has now reached Grafton Regis in Northamptonshire still on the Grand Union Canal on the afternoon of 9 July, 2010. *Victoria* is now paired with butty *Ara*, instead of *Archimedes*. Working boat *Victoria* is an Associated Canal Carriers Ltd (a subsidiary of the GUCC) motor boat Royalty class, fleet number 97, built by Yarwoods of Northwich in 1931 with a steel hull. The butty *Ara* is a Star class boat built by Harland & Wolff at Woolwich, London, in 1935, GUCC fleet number 213. It came into British Waterways ownership in 1948, then the *Willow Wren* CTS from 1963 to 1970, private ownership thereafter, original with an extended cabin.

At Grafton Regis on 9 July, 2010, is a loaded single working boat *Callisto* a GUCC motor boat Star class, built by Harland & Wolff at Woolwich, London, in 1935, fleet number 21, with a steel composite hull.

Grafton Regis from a farm access bridge over the Grand Union Canal. *Archimedes* the 1935 motor Star class working boat heads towards Braunston on the afternoon of 9 July, 2010, now singled, the butty *Ara* in the hands of *Victoria*. It appears that *Archimedes* had rubbish caught in its prop reducing speed and *Victoria* took over *Ara*.

Opposite: *Archimedes* heading away from the camera at Grafton Regis on 9 July, 2010, and towards Braunston in Northamptonshire, home of the well-known Braunston Marina.

Themis, the 1935 GUCC motor boat Star class, heads north towards Braunston at Grafton Regis on the afternoon of 9 July, 2010, heavily laden with gravel and working singly.

The only surviving original steam driven canal narrow boat *President* and her butty *Kildare* steam through the village of Handsacre on the Trent and Mersey Canal on 22 April, 2012. The *President* was built at a cost of £600 in 1909 at the Fellows, Morton & Clayton's company works at Saltley, Birmingham, and was constructed with riveted wrought iron sides and a 3" elm bottom. *President* and *Kildare* are owned by and reside at the Dudley Black Country Living Museum, and are operated by the Friends of NB *President*. The boat steamed until 1925, was motorised until the 1970s, and then steam plant was fitted again. The current engine is a 1950s' W. Sisson & Co single and the boiler the recently fitted NEI internal combustion RT Scotch type. The Trent and Mersey Canal was the boat's stamping ground when owned by British Waterways maintenance fleet.

President and *Kildare* steam through Fradley Woods on the Trent and Mersey Canal. *Kildare* is an FMC 1912-built Braithwaite and Kirk butty with iron composite hull, fleet number 274. When with Willow Wren CTS she was renamed *Snipe*.

Opposite: *President* and *Kildare* steam away from the camera at Fradley Woods on the Trent and Mersey Canal. The Fellows, Morton & Clayton livery is clearly represented in the set of images taken on the 22 April, 2012. The steam boat took part in the 2012 Queen's Jubilee Thames Parade.

The next few images are at the annual tug boat gathering at the Dudley Black Country Living Museum (BCLM) on 5 May, 2012. Taken looking down the Dudley Canal with the arm of the canal in the museum's premises and the preserved works buildings in the background is tug boat *Reginald*. This tug was built in 1887, of riveted iron construction. This 45 foot boat was originally a Stewarts & Lloyds fleet joey cargo boat, but cut down and converted to a tug in 1980. Stewarts & Lloyds were steel manufacturers of Bilston, who operated a fleet of narrow boats on the Birmingham Canal Navigation (BCN). They became part of British Steel on the 1967 nationalisation of the steel industry.

Also at the BCLM on the 5 May, 2012, is the icebreaker *Governor*. This tug was built in 1941 by Harris Brothers of Bumble Hole, Netherton, of iron construction and is 45 feet long, engined by Gardiner, and operated by Matty & Sons of Coseley in the Black Country.

A line-up of tugs on the museum's arm of the Dudley Canal, looking towards the rebuilt historic buildings and a typical nineteenth century Black Country street, crossing the canal.

An example at the BCLM of a working narrow boat in need of restoration. This particular boat is an ancient icebreaker, name or history not known. Many of the boats in this book were found in this state and lovingly restored by their owners.

Amongst the line-up of tugs at the BCLM on 5 May, 2012, is icebreaker *Nansen* built in 1957 by Yarwoods of Northwich, of iron construction and 40 feet long. This was a British Waterways towing tug, originally with a centre wheelhouse, and engined by a Lister HR 3-cylinder engine.

Another of the Stewarts & Lloyds fleet at the BCLM gathering on 5 May, 2012, is *Pacific No. 4*, an icebreaker built in 1934 by Yarwoods of Northwich, of riveted iron construction, 40 feet long and engined by a Lister HR 3-cylinder engine. This was an ex-Matty & Sons of Coseley boat that was involved in dredging contracts for the Birmingham Canal Navigation (BCN).

Taken from the canal bridge at the BCLM on 5 May, 2012, and on the left amongst the other tugs is the icebreaker *Tardebigge*, built in 1909 of iron construction, 37 feet long, and worked for the Birmingham Canal Navigation from Hawne Basin in Halesowen. A reconstructed boat from historic vessel *Antila* cut in two and the stern converted by British Waterways to a tug, and re-united in 1997. The name is taken from the Tardebigge Locks on the Worcester and Birmingham Canal in Worcestershire.

Included amongst the images of the working boats are some illustrations of the canal architecture and machinery. Here is an example of a bridge hoist to allow access from the Dudley Canal into the museum.

Continuing the theme of canal architecture, away from the Dudley Canal, and on the Stratford upon Avon Canal, near Wilmcote, Warwickshire, is an example of a lockkeeper's cottage, originally lived in by an employee of the canal company to service the locks. Now, most lockkeepers' cottages are private dwellings of some character, though there are a few on other canals which still are used as they were intended.

At the BCLM on 5 May, 2012, the tug *Enterprise No 1* is manoeuvred by muscle power. This boat was built in 1899 as a Fellows, Morton & Clayton steam boat at their Saltley works, fleet number 47. Named *Count*, she was converted to a tug in 1950 by Ernest Thomas of Walsall. Of iron and elm construction, she is powered by a 5-cylinder Gardiner engine.

Opposite: The final image from the 2012 tug gathering at the BCLM is of tug *Coventry* heading out of the museum onto the Dudley Canal having passed under the bridge hoist pictured earlier. *Coventry* was originally an iron construction horse-drawn narrow boat built in 1935, and worked for the Coventry Canal Company, converted to a tug of just over 31 feet and powered by a Lister HR 3-cylinder engine by Harris Brothers of Bumble Hole, Netherton in the Black Country.

On the Coventry Canal on 16 May, 2012, is working narrow boat *Stanton*, a GUCC motor boat of Town class, built by Yarwoods of Northwich with a steel hull in 1936, fleet number 173. The boat did have a full length conversion in the 1970s, but this was removed in 2007. The location is Atherstone Locks, near Baddesley Bridge.

Opposite: Following *Stanton* was working narrow boat *Southern Cross* also at Atherstone Locks. This GUCC narrow boat was built in 1935 by Harland & Wolff at Woolwich, London, of iron construction. In the 1950s she was used as a pleasure craft by British Waterways named *Water Nymph* and plied the Regents Canal in London as a trip boat. She is now being restored to original carrying boat state, and looking resplendent in British Waterways livery.

Taken from the Baddesley Bridge over the Coventry Canal, with a colourful field of oil seed rape and the electrified main line railway in the background, *Southern Cross* heads towards Atherstone town.

Taken from the towpath of the Coventry Canal in Atherstone, *Southern Cross* passes some unoccupied and fast-becoming-derelict factory buildings on the side of the canal.

Braunston Marina on 24 June, 2011. Fellows, Morton & Clayton motor boat Fish class built at Yarwoods of Northwich in 1934 with an iron composite hull named *Perch* fleet number 320. This boat was in two halves but re-united after major restoration at Erewash. Here seen framed in the 1834 footbridge. Each year Braunston Marina is host to an Historic Boat Rally with over 80 boats attending. The marina is located on the crossroads of the Grand Union and Oxford Canal, and was developed at the beginning of the nineteenth century as the northern waterways depot for the then Grand Junction Canal, which became the Grand Union. There are several original buildings in use, and from the canalside entrance the original 1834 cast iron towpath bridge built by Horseley Iron Works of Tipton in the Black Country, and erected by the famous engineer Thomas Telford, is a reminder of the durability of Victorian engineering.

Also framed in the Braunston towpath bridge on 24 June, 2011 is *Ibex*, a Fellows, Morton & Clayton motor boat built by Yarwoods of Northwich in 1926 with iron composite hull, fleet number 90, here in British Waterways livery, also known as *Ibis* in the 1950s. A very differing choice of names as ibex are mountain wild goats and ibis are wading birds!

Opposite: Fellows, Morton & Clayton working boats *Emu* and *Fazeley* paired together, approach the towpath bridge and access to the Braunston Marina on 24 June, 2011. *Emu* is a Yarwoods of Northwich 1926-built motor boat of iron composite hull, fleet number 18, also worked for Willow Wren CTS where she was named *Tern*. *Fazeley* is a 1921 FMC butty built at the Saltley works.

Below: Also taken from the cast iron towpath bridge on 24 June, 2011, is this image of Fellows, Morton & Clayton working boat *Clover* a 1935-built Yarwoods of Northwich motor boat with iron composite hull and fleet number 332.

Approaching the junction with the Grand Union Canal on 24 June, 2011, on the North Oxford Canal is Grand Union Carrying Company motor boat named *Dorado*, built by Harland & Wolff of Woolwich, London, in 1935 with steel hull and fleet number 36. This boat was cut down to 45 feet when in the ownership of British Waterways for maintenance work, and is currently awaiting full restoration.

Also approaching the junction with the Grand Union Canal on 24 June, 2011, on the North Oxford Canal is Grand Union Carrying Company motor boat Town class named *Aldgate*, built by Harland & Wolff of Woolwich, London, in 1936 with a steel hull and fleet number 103. In the 1960s she was hired to Willow Wren CTS, then sold by British Waterways Board to Alfred Matty & Sons prior to preservation.

From the towpath bridge at Braunston Marina on 24 June, 2011, Fellows, Morton & Clayton motor boat *Python* built in 1929 by Yarwoods of Northwich with a coppered steel composite hull and fleet number 249. She is seen here in British Waterways livery which she carried when working for the maintenance fleet up till 2009 when she was leased to the Chesterfield Canal Trust.

Opposite: In the Bottom Lock at Braunston next to the Dry Dock building on 26 June, 2011, is Fellows, Morton & Clayton motor boat *Dove*, built by Yarwoods of Northwich in 1925 with iron composite hull, fleet number 295, engined by an Armstrong Siddeley AS2.

Opposite: At Braunston on the Grand Union Canal on 26 June, 2011, one of the preserved narrow boats of the fleet of Ovaltine boats is photographed. The popular health drink Ovaltine was invented by Dr George Wander, a Swiss chemist in 1865. His son Albert set up a company in the UK and ultimately built a factory to produce the drink at Kings Langley, near Watford, in 1913, in close proximity to the Grand Union Canal. Coal was required to fire the factory boilers and this was sourced from the Warwickshire Coalfields. A small fleet of narrow boats was purchased by Ovaltine to collect and deliver the fuel, the first commencing work in 1926 and this continued until the 1950s when coal gave way to oil.

Below: This is a general view on 26 June, 2011 of the "traffic jam" of narrow boats on the Grand Union Canal which occurs when the grand parade of boats takes place at the annual Historic Boat Rally at Braunston Marina.

On the Grand Union Canal on 26 June, 2011, is seen *Columbia* built by Yarwoods of Northwich as a Town and Country class butty of iron composite hull and converted to a motor boat in 1939, the Fellows, Morton & Clayton fleet number is 151. This boat has a chequered history in that in preservation with various owners she was shortened to 54 feet and converted to a day boat, then caught fire and sank. Later she was raised and finally renovated as a conversion to outline working boat. The lady boater is using a barge pole which is used to propel or guide a barge through water; the barge (or quant) pole is usually made of wood or hollow metal and capped and pronged at the bottom to stop it sinking into the mud. This innocent piece of equipment unfairly spawned the saying "wouldn't touch whatever with a barge pole".

Also on the Grand Union Canal on 26 June, 2011, is seen *Skylark*. This motor boat was built by Yarwoods of Northwich in 1934 of rounded chines and steel construction for the firm of Cowburn & Cowpar. This firm of Trafford Park, Manchester, had their own fleet of eight boats to deliver chemical products mainly to Courtaulds in Coventry but also to other plants. Because of the hazardous nature of some of the products, all boats had a release flood valve which allowed the boats to sink quickly if fire occurred. This continued until the mid-1950s. *Skylark* was one of the last boats to come out of service and was sold to carrier Jonathan Horsefield Ltd of Runcorn. From then on the boat was converted to a day boat; finally after several owners in 1994 the boat was restored to working trim. This boat still works for her living, delivering winter fuel on the Caldon Canal, Staffordshire.

A view of *Skylark's* cabin, and the livery of Cowburn & Cowpar of Manchester.

Approaching Bottom Lock on the Grand Union Canal at Braunston on 26 June, 2011, with boatbuilders and fitters works in the background, is the working boat *Towcester*. A Grand Union Canal Carrying Company motor boat Town class built in 1937 by Harland & Wolff of Woolwich, London, with iron composite hull, fleet number 181. This boat still works for her living – owned by JE Cook of Stoke Bruerne – and delivers fuel and other goods on the Grand Union, as can be seen from the load which *Towcester* carries.

Opposite: *Towcester* is seen unloading goods from the Braunston Bottom Lock of the Grand Union Canal for the so-called Stop House, now the Boat Shop, the original toll office next to the lock and iron side bridge, and opposite the eighteenth century Dry Dock building.

At Braunston Bottom Lock on the Grand Union Canal on 26 June, 2011, is seen the pairing of narrow boats *Phobos* and *George*. On the left is *Phobos* a Grand Union Canal Carrying Company motor boat Star class, built by Harland & Wolff of Woolwich, London, in 1935 of iron composite hull and fleet number 71. On the right obscured a little by *Phobos* is the Associated Canal Carriers Ltd (a subsidiary of the GUCC) motor boat Royalty class of 1929 named *George* built by the Steel Barrel Company of Uxbridge, Middlesex, and fleet number 46. Phobos is a satellite of Mars, named after a mythological Greek god.

On the Grand Union Canal on 26 June, 2011, is *Cassiopeia*, a Grand Union Canal Carrying Company's motor boat Star class built by Harland & Wolff of Woolwich, London, in 1935 of iron composite hull and fleet number 23. *Cassiopeia* (a constellation in the northern sky and named after a queen in Greek mythology) is seen here in British Waterways livery, with the eighteenth-century Braunston Dry Dock building on the right in the background, having just cleared Bottom Lock.

Also on the Grand Union Canal on 26 June, 2011, having just cleared Braunston Bottom Lock is Fellows, Morton & Clayton ex-steam narrow boat, named *Marquis*, built at FMC Saltley works as part of the steam fleet in 1898, of iron composite hull and fleet number 237. The steamer was converted to diesel power in 1925.

At Little Braunston Lock number 2 with the canal cottage on the right is *Cassiopeia*. In front of the boat are four more locks and Braunston Tunnel, opened in 1796 to bore through the Northamptonshire heights: it is 2042 yards long (just over a mile long).

Opposite: At Hillmorton Locks near Rugby on the Oxford Canal on the evening of 26 June, 2011, is seen an ancient Birmingham Canal Navigation joey named *Seal*, currently under restoration as can be seen from the brown undercoat, eventually to become a tug boat.

Opposite: Also at Hillmorton Locks on the Oxford Canal on 26 June, 2011, going home from Braunston is Fellows, Morton & Clayton 1926-built motor boat *Ibex* in British Waterways livery.

Below: Finally at Hillmorton Locks on 26 June, 2011, is seen Grand Union Canal Carrying Company motor boat Town class, named *Darley* built by Harland & Wolff in 1937, hull of steel and fleet number 135. This boat was cut in two at Alfred Matty's in the late 1960s for use as a dredger, but later re-assembled in the 1980s.

At the eastern portal of the 2042-yard long Braunston Tunnel, near Welton village and wharf, the tug *Baltic* emerges into the morning sunlight of 27 June, 2011. *Baltic* is a Birmingham Canal Navigation icebreaker, built circa 1840 with iron hull and originally horse drawn, a remarkable survivor which was sold to the British Waterways Board in the early 1970s, then motorised and converted in 1977/8.

Also at the Braunston Tunnel eastern portal on 27 June, 2011, *Dodona* emerges into the sunlight and heads for Welton Wharf. *Dodona* is a Grand Union Canal Carrying Company butty boat Star class, now motorised, built by Harland & Wolff in 1935 of steel composite hull and fleet number 269.

The Transport Trust honoured the canals in 2012, and a heritage 'Red Wheel' awarded to historic sites was affixed to the top lock of the Hatton Flight on the Grand Union Canal, near Warwick. The award, one of five canal awards, was given to mark the important role of Britain's inland waterways in the development of transport and the Industrial Revolution. The plaque was unveiled by Tony Hales, CBE, then Chairman of British Waterways on the left and Sir William McAlpine Bt, President of the Transport Trust on the right. Also present was Peter Stone of the Trust.

Near Newbold on Avon on the Oxford Canal on 13 June, 2012, *Callisto* a Grand Union Canal Carrying Company motor boat Star class, built by Harland & Wolff of Woolwich, London, in 1935, fleet number 21, with steel composite hull, heads towards Rugby with a load of fuel to deliver to canalside dwellers.

At Newbold on Avon on the Oxford Canal on 13 June, 2012, the only original steam narrow boat *President* and butty *Kildare* steam round the bend in the canal. *President* was built in 1909 for the Fellows, Morton & Clayton carriers, and was part of a fleet of 31 steamers that flourished between 1889 and 1931.

At Newbold on Avon, near Rugby on 13 June, 2012, *President* and *Kildare* are tied up for a lunch stop.

Whilst strictly not historic working boats, apart from President, the following fifteen images are of steam driven narrow boats, some replicas and new builds, but also original or adapted boats. The first four are images of the steam boats sailing towards the first annual steam boat gathering at Swan Lane Boatyard on the Coventry Canal, held on the weekend of 15 to 17 June, 2012. This image is of steam boat Adamant, on the Oxford Canal, on the western side of Ansty village, and about to head towards Hawkesbury Junction and then the Coventry Canal on 14 June, 2012.

Adamant moves away to head towards Hawkesbury Junction. The hull is original from around 1897 and from a BCN joey, and she is classed as a canal tunnel tug. The engine fitted is a c.1895 Cochrane & Co Ltd 2-crank compound, and the boiler was built by Abels Shipbuilders Ltd of Bristol in 1988.

On 14 June, 2012, on the eastern side of Ansty village on the Oxford Canal and heading towards Hawkesbury Junction and the steam boat gathering on the Coventry Canal, is new-build of 2006 steam narrow boat named *Trevor*.

Opposite: The 1909 steam narrow boat *President* and butty *Kildare* are seen at Ansty on the Oxford Canal on 14 June, 2012, heading for Hawkesbury Junction and the steam boat gathering on the Coventry Canal.

On 15 June, 2012, Swan Lane Boatyard, at Stoke Heath, Coventry, is home to some of the participants at the steam boat gathering on the Coventry Canal. On the far left in the image and next to the steam boats – and by way of a comparison – is pleasure craft nb *Coventrian* which is used as a floating classroom for local schoolchildren and other events.

A tight fit! The chimney is dropped just in time on 1986-built steam boat *Tixall* as she heads for the boatyard and the steam boat gathering and sails under Red Lane New Bridge, Stoke Heath, Coventry, on the Coventry Canal on 15 June, 2012.

The engine room on steam boat *Tixall*. The hull was built by Stoke on Trent Boatbuilders in 1986, the engine is a 1986 Anthony Bever of Swindon model AA Leek Compound, and boiler is a 1985 JO Lugg & Son Ltd of Billinghurst, Sussex, Lune Valley WT type. The boat is named after Tixall village on the Staffordshire and Worcestershire Canal.

On Saturday 16 June, 2012, the convoy of steam boats headed for Hawkesbury Junction on the Coventry Canal and in the short tunnel under the Heath Crescent Bridge built in 1996 over the canal is seen replica Braunston canal tunnel steam tug named *Hasty*. This faithful recreation, still requiring some internal fittings to complete, has a hull built by Brinklow Boat Services, the engine is a 1965 Sissons of Gloucester repatriated from South Africa and the boiler a 1992 Fulton of Bristol Classic Steam.

Opposite: On 16 June, 2012, the steam narrow boat *Whistle Down the Wind* exits Heath Crescent Bridge on the Coventry Canal. The name is based on the 1961 cult film "Whistle Down the Wind" from a novel by Mary Hayley Bell, and a subsequent musical.

On 16 June, 2012, on the Coventry Canal and in the short tunnel under the Heath Crescent Bridge, Stoke Heath, Coventry, is seen 1991-built steam narrow boat *Emily Anne*. A later image shows the boat with a tall cabin, which has been demounted to clear the tunnel.

Another view of Swan Lane Boatyard, Stoke Heath, Coventry, on the Coventry Canal, on Sunday 17 June, 2012, showing steam boats *Hasty*, *Whistle Down the Wind* and *Trevor*.

On the canal-side of the Coventry Canal next to the boatyard on 17 June, 2012, is seen the 1991-built steam narrow boat *Emily Anne* of Stroud, Gloucestershire. The hull was built by Watercraft, the engine is a 1991 Anthony Bever of Swindon AA Leek Compound and the boiler a 1991 Langley Engineering VFT type. The cabin which was demounted for the tunnel is in situ in this image.

Sunday 17 June, 2012, saw the convoy of steam boats depart Swan Lane Boatyard for the terminus of the Coventry Canal, the Bishop Street Basin, in the centre of the city. Here steam boat *Hasty* passes the ex-Royal Navy Ordnance Factory on the west side of the Coventry Canal, which apparently in its heyday was the longest factory building in the country.

At Bishop Street Basin on the Coventry Canal, on 17 June, 2012, the steam boat *Laplander* is seen manoeuvrering in the basin having just arrived. *Laplander* is an icebreaker tug. The hull was built in the Birmingham area c.1830 and made of riveted iron; she is a four berth, cabin forward, tiller steering boat. The engine is a Bailey Single, formerly a non-condensing stationery engine, and the boiler is a 1960s-built Clarkson, fitted in 1998 and fuelled by either kerosene or recycled oil. *Laplander* was originally a horse-drawn boat, taken into the Birmingham Canal Navigation as an icebreaker, and listed in 1858. Later fitted with a Bolinder IC engine, she was converted to steam by the current owner. Other boats in the class were named after Arctic exploration, not originally as the boats as built pre-date that era, but during their long lives, ie *Shackleton*, *Antarctica* and *Oates*.

Approaching the Bishop Street Basin on the Coventry Canal, and passing under the Drapers Field Bridge on 17 June, 2012, is steam boat *Trevor*. The basin was much modernised in the 1980s, but still retains the façade and fabric of the 1914 wooden canal warehouses, themselves built on the site of the original eighteenth century warehouses. The old Weighbridge Office is preserved and is now an information centre. In the central area of the basin is a statue of the famous canal engineer James Brindley.

Something a little bit different, but still canal related. On 19 June, 2012, the National Steam Car Association visited the Leighton Buzzard area, and here 1904 Stanley CX steam car with tiller steering is posed just outside Grove Lock on the Grand Union Canal, with a maintenance boat in the foreground.

The 2012 gathering of historic narrow boats at Braunston Marina. On 20 June, 2012, narrow boat *Vesta* approaches the 1834 cast iron towpath bridge at the entrance of the marina from the Grand Union Canal in the company of two swans. *Vesta* is a Grand Union Canal Carrying Company motor boat Star class built in 1935 by Harland & Wolff of Woolwich, London, of iron composite hull and fleet number 96. Worked for Stanton Ironworks of Ilkeston, Derbyshire, as Stanton no. 61 in 1941, then in Stewarts & Lloyds of Bilston ownership in 1947 she was shortened to become a tug number 3 in the fleet.

Opposite: *Vesta* enters the Braunston Marina having passed under the Horseley Ironworks towpath bridge.

Below: On 20 June, 2012, narrow boat *Panther* approaches Braunston on the Oxford Canal, having just passed under Navigation Bridge, Willoughby, which can be seen in the background. *Panther* is a Fellows, Morton & Clayton motor boat built by Yarwoods of Northwich in 1929 of steel composite hull and fleet number 250. *Panther* is in the hands of the Coventry Canal Society.

Opposite: This narrow boat looks lifesize at first glance. However, this is a superbly constructed quarter size model of Fellows, Morton & Clayton narrow boat *Eagle*, radio controlled, with a model Bolinder engine. At Braunston Marina on 24 June, 2012.

Below: At Braunston on 24 June, 2012, on the Grand Union Canal and having just passed under bridge 91 which carries the A45 Trunk Road over the canal, is narrow boat *Barrow*, a Grand Union Canal Carrying Company motor boat Town class, built by Harland & Wolff in 1936 with steel hull and fleet number 125, sold to the British Waterways Board in 1967/8.

Heading towards Braunston on 24 June, 2012, away from the Braunston Turn junction with the Oxford Canal, and the two cast iron Horseley Ironworks bridges over the two canals, is narrow boat *Aquilla*. She is a Grand Union Canal Carrying Company motor boat Star class built by Harland & Wolff of Woolwich, London, in 1935 of iron composite hull and fleet number 10, currently an under cloth conversion.

Taking the Oxford Canal at Braunston Turn on 24 June, 2012, is narrow boat *Corona*. She is a Grand Union Canal Carrying Company motor boat Star class built by Harland & Wolff of Woolwich, London, in 1935 of steel composite hull and fleet number 32. *Corona* is named after the celestial atmosphere of the sun.

Also taking the Oxford Canal away from Braunston on 24 June, 2012, is narrow boat *Admiral*, a Fellows, Morton & Clayton originally steam narrow boat, built in 1905 at FMC Saltley works, Birmingham, with a John Thompson boiler and Haines engine. *Admiral* was converted to a motor boat in 1924 and a Bolinder 15hp type NE fitted. The coal carrying company Samuel Barlow of Glascote on the Coventry Canal, which later in 1931 had offices in Birmingham, bought *Admiral* in 1942, and this is the livery currently being carried. In 1965 the boat was shortened and converted to a pleasure boat, but has now been re-converted to a working boat. Samuel Barlow was founded in 1870 to carry coal from the Warwickshire coalfields to London; the fleet was upwards of 100 boats at one time. In the 1940s this had become around 70 boats, but the company ceased trading in 1961. The boat now has a butty, the ex-FMC *Verbena*, built at FMC Saltley works as an Overseas class butty and fleet number 203, also named *Vienna*.

Opposite: Later on 24 June, 2012, at Hillmorton, near Rugby, to the east of the locks, is narrow boat *Auriga* approaching Moors Bridge 72 on the Oxford Canal. She is a Grand Union Carrying Company motor boat Star class built by Harland & Wolff of Woolwich, London, in 1935 of iron composite hull and fleet number 17. In British Waterways ownership she was employed on the maintenance fleet on the Trent & Mersey Canal. Currently under restoration, *Auriga* is named after a constellation which translates from the Latin as charioteer.

Late afternoon at Hillmorton Locks numbers 2 and 3 on 24 June, 2012, is seen narrow boat *Lamprey*. She is a Fellows, Morton & Clayton motor boat Fish class built by Yarwoods of Northwich in 1934 of iron composite hull and fleet number 316. *Lamprey* is named after a type of freshwater eel.

Opposite: At Hillmorton Locks 6 and 7 is icebreaker tug *Laplander* on 24 June, 2012. The hull was built in Birmingham c.1830, and whilst originally horse-drawn, and then diesel engined, she has been steam driven since 1998. The radio station masts at Hillmorton can be seen behind the locks.

At Hillmorton Locks 6 and 7 is icebreaker tug *Baltic* on 24 June, 2012. A Birmingham Canal Navigation icebreaker, built c.1840 with iron hull, originally horse drawn, motorised and converted in 1977/8.

At Hillmorton Locks 6 and 7 is narrow boat *Hadley* on 24 June, 2012. A Grand Union Canal Carrying Company motor boat Town class, built by Harland & Wolff of Woolwich, London, in 1937 of steel hull construction and fleet number 147. Note use of barge pole. The radio station masts are very clear in this image.

At Hillmorton, to the east of the locks on 24 June, 2012, is seen the tug *White Heather*. She is a service vessel canal tug, built by JS Watson of Gainsborough at Beckenham on the Trent for the Borough of St Marylebone in 1932 as a refuse tug. In British Waterways ownership she was used on maintenance. *White Heather* currently is engined by a Ford 6-cylinder 120 hp engine. She is one of only 4 round bilge canal tugs in existence, and took part in the Queen's Jubilee Thames Pageant.

Opposite: A reminder of the state of the majority of working narrow boats before restoration, this was seen at the Dudley Black Country Living Museum on 14 July, 2012. The boat is named *Birchill* after a suburb of Walsall, and was a former Ernest Thomas of Walsall Day Boat.

On the Grand Union Canal at Stoke Hammond Bridge 106 on 27 July, 2012, are *Nutfield* and butty *Raymond*. *Nutfield* is a Grand Union Canal Carrying Company motor boat Town class built by Yarwoods of Northwich in 1938 with a steel hull. *Raymond* is a Samuel Barlow Coal Carrying Company butty built by Nursers of Braunston in 1958 of wood construction and fleet number 42, last one built, also worked for Blue Line of Braunston, successors to Barlows. The "Friends of *Raymond*" restore and run both boats, as they were original pairings.

At Soulbury Three Locks on the Grand Union Canal on 27 July, 2012, *Nutfield* and *Raymond* are side by side as they pass through the locks.

Nutfield and *Raymond* are at Old Linslade on the Grand Union Canal as they head for Leighton Buzzard on 27 July, 2012.

On 27 July, 2012, tug *Sickle* followed the pair through Old Linslade on the Grand Union Canal. *Sickle* started life as a Grand Union Canal Carrying Company motor boat Star class built by Yarwoods of Northwich in 1937 of rounded chines and steel hull construction and fleet number 84. In 1942 the boat was shortened, and has now been rebuilt as a tug in British Waterways livery.

On 27 July, 2012, on the Grand Union Canal approaching Leighton Buzzard, the tug *Sickle* is seen at Old Linslade at the former wharf next to Sand 'Oles Bridge 110. The bridge is so called because sand was loaded here from a quarry about two miles away, carried by horse and cart, which ceased in the early 1950s. The elecrified West Coast Main Line Railway is close to the canal at this point.

Opposite: A departure from the canals of England, this image is of the Bottom Lock of the Caledonian Canal in the West Highlands of Scotland. The Caledonian Canal was completed in 1822, the Principal Engineer being the celebrated Thomas Telford. It starts at Inverness on the east coast and 62 miles miles later ends at Loch Eil, Corpach near Fort William on the west coast. Leading to Loch Eil is 'Neptune's Staircase' of eight locks and the Banavie Swingbridge for the road and Fort William to Mallaig Railway line. The boats pictured on 15 October, 2010 have taken advantage of the maximum size of 150 feet (10.7 metres) ruling on the canal which is over double that on the English canals, though still controlled by British Waterways, now Scottish Canals. The first boat in the image is the *Hjalmar Bjorge* of Stornoway, the largest town in the Outer Hebrides.

Below: At the eastern side of Ansty village on the Oxford Canal on 1 April, 2010, is Fellows, Morton & Clayton motor boat *Plover*, built by FMC Saltley works in 1915 with an iron composite hull and fleet number 94. British Waterways renamed the boat *Parrot* in 1952, but in preservation has reverted back to *Plover*. The boat has had four engines in her life, starting with a Bolinder 15 hp, then in the 1960s firstly a Royal Enfield Horizontal Opposed then an Armstrong Siddeley Merganser Twin. Currently fitted in 1988 is a Lister JP3.

Plover heads away from Bridge 16 in the village of Ansty on the Oxford Canal on 1 April, 2010, and towards Hawkesbury Junction and the Coventry Canal, crossing a pleasure boat as she does so.

Following on behind *Plover* at Ansty on the Oxford Canal on 1 April, 2010, is Fellows, Morton & Clayton motor boat named *Hare*, built by Yarwoods of Northwich in 1926 with iron composite hull and fleet number 71. This boat was cut into two parts by British Waterways in their ownership in the 1950s and part used as a hire boat called *Walter Bullrush*, but then re-lengthened.

Opposite: This is Bridge 46 to the west of Gayton Junction on the Grand Union Canal; the junction is with the Grand Union Main and the Northampton Arm of the canal, next to the electrified main railway line, and a few miles south of Northampton. On 30 September, 2011, Grand Union Canal Carrying Company motor boat Town class named *Purton*, built by Yarwoods of Northwich in 1936 with steel hull and fleet number 165, heads towards the junction.

Below: The working boat *Renfrew* is framed in Bridge 46 at Gayton Junction on the Grand Union Canal on 30 September, 2011. *Renfrew* is a Grand Union Canal Carrying Company motor boat Town class, built by Yarwoods of Northwich in 1936 with a hull of steel and fleet number 165. She was shortened in 1960 whilst in the ownership of British Waterways.

This is *Renfrew* shortly after the previous image as she heads towards Gayton Junction on the Grand Union Canal on 30 September, 2011.

South of Gayton Junction at Bridge 49 Station Road on the Grand Union Canal on 30 September, 2011, is seen the pairing of *Nutfield* and butty *Raymond* working south.

A close up view of butty *Raymond* at Bridge 49 Station Road, Gayton. Note banner advertising the "Friends of *Raymond*". Behind the boats is the electrified main line railway bridge.

On the Worcester and Birmingham Canal at Tardebigge Wharf, near Bromsgrove, on 8 October, 2010 is stabled converted narrow boat *Adder*, originally a Fellows, Morton & Clayton motor boat built by Yarwoods of Northwich in 1923 of iron composite hull and fleet number 285. The Worcester and Birmingham Canal was commenced in 1792 and completed in 1815, starting at Worcester with an outlet to the River Severn to Gas Street Basin in Birmingham, 29 miles(47 km) in length, with 58 locks including the Tardebigge Flight. A major user was Cadburys of Bournville.

A view of Tardebigge Wharf on the Worcester and Birmingham Canal. This is a British Waterways Maintenance Depot, and the canal reached here in 1807 as a temporary terminus for trading into Worcester. The wharf is situated at Top Lock on the Tardebigge Flights, the longest flight of locks in the country. There are 30 in total on a two and one quarter mile stretch, raising the canal 220 feet up to Tardebigge Tunnel (580 yards). A blue plaque commemorates the meeting near here of LTC (Tom) Rolt and Robert Aikman in 1945 aboard Tom Rolt's boat *Cressie* and the founding a year later of the Inland Waterways Association and the start of the canal restoration movement.

I doubt if there is a finer backdrop of any canal in the world, than the Corpach end of the Caledonian Canal. A sailing boat exits the canal into Loch Eil. The highest mountain in the British Isles, Ben Nevis, at 4409feet (1344metres), towers above Loch Eil, part of the Grampian Mountains in the Lochaber District of the Scottish Highlands. This image was taken in the late afternoon on 16 October, 2010. If the whole canal is used there are 29 locks to navigate, 4 aqueducts and 10 bridges. Only a third of the canal was man-made, the rest is through Loch Dochfor, Loch Ness, Loch Oich, and Loch Lochy all of which form the 'Great Glen'.

The next few images are of the "Jam 'Ole Run" which took place from 16 to 23 October, 2010. This run using original working boats re-enacts the last regular long distance coal haulage by canal. Coal was taken from Baddesley Colliery, near Atherstone on the Coventry Canal, via the Oxford Canal at Hawkesbury Junction, via the Grand Union Canal to Kearley & Tonge's Jam Factory at Southall. It was made by the Samuel Barlow Coal Carrying Company at first, then by their successors Blue Line Canal Carriers. The last run was in October, 1970, hence the run on this 40th anniversary. The basin which was used for the unloading of coal by Kearley & Tonge's Jam Factory was Mitre Docks, on the Paddington Arm of the Grand Union. The length of the run is around 250 miles, with approximately 200 locks, which shows this was no easy work for the crews who were paid by the tonnage carried. Canal trade had declined drastically by the 1960s and together with financial difficulties at the jam factory and lack of maintenance on the canal infrastructure and the boats, and of course, road competition, meant that the end came in 1970, ending two centuries of coal to London by canal. Here at Hopton Locks and Wharf south of Leighton Buzzard on the Grand Union Canal on the 22 October, 2010, are working boats *Corona* and *Renfrew* taking part in the run.

At Grove Lock at Leighton Buzzard on the Grand Union Canal on 22 October, 2010, working boat *Victoria* runs through the lock on the "Jam 'Ole Run" with a pleasure boat. *Victoria* is an Associated Canal Carrying Company (a subsidiary of the GUCCC) motor boat, Royalty class, built by Yarwoods in 1931 with a steel hull and fleet number 97. She also carried the name *Linda* in the 1960s, and was restored in the early 1970s.

At Grove Lock on the "Jam 'Ole Run" on the Grand Union Canal on 22 October, 2010. On the left is the bow of *Corona* and on the right is *Renfrew* a Grand Union Canal Carrying Company motor boat Town class built by Yarwoods of Northwich in 1936 with a steel hull and fleet number 165.

On the "Jam 'Ole Run" on 22 October, 2010, at Soulbury Three Locks on the Grand Union Canal, side by side in the lock are *Stanton* and *Dove*. *Stanton* is a Grand Union Canal Carrying Company motor boat Town class built by Yarwoods of Northwich in 1936 with a steel hull and fleet number 173. *Dove* was originally the butty *Aldersley* built by the Severn & Canal Carrying Company (SCCC) at Gloucester in 1913 of wood construction. The boat was converted to motor boat no. 8 in 1929 by the SCCC with a Bolinder engine. The boat was then owned by Thomas Clayton of Oldbury and named *Dove* in 1948.

Opposite: On the "Jam 'Ole Run" on 22 October, 2010, on the Grand Union Canal *Victoria* exits Lock 3 and heads towards Fenny Stratford with the canalside inn the Grand Union in the background.

It is the turn of *Corona* and *Renfrew* to pass through the Soulbury Locks side by side, passing the canalside inn the Grand Union.

On 22 October, 2010, working boat *Ascot* pauses at Fenny Lock at Fenny Stratford on the Grand Union Canal. This boat delivered fuel and goods to the canalside dwellers and was well loaded. Currently as at January, 2013 the boat is no longer used in that context and is up for sale. *Ascot* is a Grand Union Canal Carrying Company motor boat Town class built by Harland & Wolff of Woolwich in 1936 with fleet number 104. After British Waterways ownership the boat was hired to Willow Wren CTS in the mid-1960s, then to private owners.

On 22 October, 2010, *Ascot* passes *Purton* going north on the "Jam 'Ole Run". *Purton* is a Grand Union Canal Carrying Company motor boat Town class built by Yarwoods of Northwich in 1936. At Fenny Lock there are some canalside cottages, a swing bridge, a public house and in the backgoround is the Bedford to Bletchley railway line.

The Tug Boat Gathering at the Dudley Black Country Living Museum on 3 May, 2010. This is the first general view of the arm of the Dudley Canal in which the tug boats gather, within the museum. This first image shows the layout of the arm with the Dudley Canal just discernable on the right, the restored buildings in the centre, with the street behind, and on the left the tugs leading to the canal bridge.

A closer view of the tugs on the Dudley Canal Arm in the Black Country Living Museum.

On the Dudley Arm of the Dudley Canal on 3 May, 2010, is icebreaker tug named *Sharpness*, built in 1908 with a steel hull. This type of icebreaker was built specifically for the Worcester & Birmingham Canal, the River Severn and the Gloucester & Sharpness Ship Canal, originally with a Kromhout 30 hp petrol/kerosene engine, but replaced with a 1932 Gardner 422 diesel engine.

At the Black Country Living Museum at the Tug Gathering on 3 May, 2010, there is a demonstration of loading of goods, in this case a wooden crate, on to a joey boat from the 1960 Morris Commercial LC5 of Canal & Vehicle Services by mechanical crane.

Here the demonstration continues and the wooden crate is about to be loaded on to the joey boat.

Opposite: Each year on the first weekend in September the Shackerstone Festival takes place. This is a celebration of road, rail and water-borne transport. Shackerstone village in Leicestershire is doubly fortunate in that the Ashby Canal passes through and it is the headquarters of the preserved Battlefield Line. The festival is supported by the villagers, the Shackerstone Railway Society and the Ashby Canal Association. On the canal a number of historic boats attend, and the day after the festival, Monday 3 September, 2012, many head away from Shackerstone. In this image the converted working boat *Elizabeth* sails south on the Ashby Canal. This boat was originally a Fellows, Morton & Clayton iron butty and horse-drawn. After sale in 1936 she was converted to the outline seen and named *Elizabeth*, with currently (from 1988) a Gardner 2LW engine fitted.

Departing Shackerstone on the Ashby Canal on 3 September, 2012, is *Swift* a Cowburn & Cowpar of Trafford Park, Manchester, motor boat built by Yarwoods of Northwich in 1933 with steel composite hull. The chemical products company which employed a fleet of 8 boats still exists but unfortunately does not use the canals for transport these days.

Whilst at Stoke Golding on the Ashby Canal awaiting the arrival of the working boats from Shackerstone on 3 September, 2012, this delightful steam launch named *Chantilly* sailed by. This steam launch has a Steam & Electric Launch Company hull, the engine is a John Tilley compound, and the boiler is a 1988 Langley Engineering Kingdom VFT type.

The next half a dozen images of working boats were taken at Stoke Golding on the Ashby Canal on 3 September, 2012. First narrow boat seen was *Kestrel*, a Fellows, Morton & Clayton motor boat built by Yarwoods of Northwich in 1928 of iron composite hull and fleet number 202. She was cut into two boats by British Waterways in 1959, the stern remaining as *Kestrel*, the other boat resulting called *Water Lily*. She is now restored to her former state. *Kestrel* is towing narrow boat *Northolt* at this point, and note "Coal for Sale" on *Kestrel's* bowfront.

Opposite: Being towed by *Kestrel* is *Northolt* which is an ancient narrow boat built in 1897 and traded for Samuel Barlow Coal Carrying Company of Birmingham for many years before being taken over by Fellows, Morton & Clayton. In 1943 she took part in the wartime film "Painted Boats" and was renamed *Sunny Valley* which title it kept until 2009 before a new owner reverted back to *Northolt*. She was a Birmingham Canal Navigation registered boat.

At Stoke Golding on the Ashby Canal on 3 September, 2012, is *Ariel*. This is a former Grand Union Canal Carrying working narrow boat, part-converted.

At Stoke Golding on the Ashby Canal on 3 September, 2012, is *Python* a Fellows, Morton & Clayton motor boat built by Yarwoods of Northwich in 1929 of coppered steel hull and fleet number 249, in British Waterways livery, now leased to Chesterfield Canal Trust.

Following *Python* at Stoke Golding was *Badger* a Fellows, Morton & Clayton motor boat built by Yarwoods of Northwich in 1923 of iron composite hull and fleet number 288, in FMC livery.

At Stoke Golding on the Ashby Canal on 3 September, 2012, is *Darley*. This is a Grand Union Canal Carrying Company motor boat Town class built by Harland & Wolff of Woolwich, London, in 1937 of steel hull and fleet number 135. *Darley* was cut into two by Alfred Matty in the 1960s for use as a dredger, but re-assembled in 1983. Seen here in British Waterways livery.

Seen here at Dadlington Bridge 28 on the Ashby Canal on 3 September, 2012, is *Swift* a Cowburn & Cowpar motor boat built by Yarwoods of Northwich in 1933 of steel composite hull, in the livery of the company.

Opposite: Approaching Factory Junction, Tipton Green, on the Dudley Canal on 8 January, 2011, working for real and icebreaking on the frozen canal is tug icebreaker *Bittell*. The icebreaker *Bittell* was built in 1934 by Yarwoods of Northwich and Harris Bros with riveted iron hull for Stewarts & Lloyds of Bilston's fleet for which she was number 5. Originally engined by a Fordson 4-cylinder tractor engine, now a Lister HA 3-cylinder. Also with the British Waterways Board, but carrying the Stewarts & Lloyds livery. The ice was being cleared in order that the narrow boat *Sagitta* could visit a boatyard for maintenance work to be carried out, from the Dudley Black Country Living Museum.

Below: *Bittell* now working hard and icebreaking on the Birmingham Level Main Line Canal, on 8 January, 2011. She has just cleared the three locks at Factory Junction. Note the crew earning their living.

At the opposite end of 2011, on 3 December, narrow boat *Panther* is seen on the Oxford Canal at Brinklow, with the electrified main line railway in the background. *Panther* is a Fellows, Morton & Clayton motor boat built by Yarwoods of Northwich in 1929 of steel composite hull and fleet number 250. She is looked after by the Coventry Canal Society.

There are several places in the country where the railways and the canals coincide. Of course, these two competitors did work together and ultimately the railways in many instances took over the canals. By way of illustration here at Brinklow on 3 December, 2011, passing the Oxford Canal with a moored pleasure boat in the foreground, is preserved steam railway locomotive 70000 'Britannia' at speed on the electrified main line and on an excursion heading for Chester. The steam very nearly coincided with working boat *Panther* which came through a few minutes beforehand, seen in the previous image.

Back to the first part of 2011, and on 8 January, the ice has been cleared on the Birmingham Level Main Line Canal at Tipton, by the icebreaker tug *Bittell*. The Grand Union Canal Carrying Company motor boat Small Northwich Star class built by Yarwoods of Northwich in 1935 with iron composite hull and fleet number 80 named *Sagitta* passes the Tipton Railway Station (in the background) on her way to Caggy's Boatyard for maintenance work to be carried out. *Sagitta* is kept by the Dudley Canal Trust, next to the Dudley Black Country Living Museum. Sagitta is a constellation in the Milky Way and translates from the Latin as Arrow.

On the 8 January, 2011, at Caggy's Boatyard, Tipton, situated on the Birmingham Level Main Line Canal, occupying the entrance to the former Toll End Communication Canal and Tipton Green Branch, is the tug boat *Caggy*. A commuter train charges by on the railway line. *Caggy* is an icebreaker tug built in 1944, owned by the late Alan Stevens of Tipton and proprietor of Caggy's Boatyard, and worked on the Birmingham Canal Navigation. She is 44 feet long with currently a Lister JP 3-cylinder engine fitted.

Sandbach is based on a Yarwoods of Northwich tug boat, and is pictured on 25 June, 2010 at Hillmorton, near Rugby, on the Oxford Canal, in London, Midland & Scottish (LMS) Railway colours. The LMS inherited a considerable number of canals and boats from the constituent companies on the railway company grouping in 1923. They also commissioned a fleet of new boats from Yarwoods of Northwich in 1928, mainly for interchange work on the Birmingham Canal Navigation.

At the newly restored Droitwich Barge Canal in Droitwich Town on 8 April, 2012, moored up is one of the fleet of the Ovaltine Company of Kings Langley, a coal carrier boat, now under conversion.

At Hillmorton Locks on 25 June, 2010, going south on the Oxford Canal is narrow boat *Whitby*, a Grand Union Canal Carrying Company motor boat Town class built by Yarwoods of Northwich in 1937 of steel hull and fleet number 185.

A detail from a working boat cabin, showing the type of decoration favoured by the canal community, also seen on utensils, water cans, etc. Note the oil lamp in the cabin.

Opposite: The Droitwich Barge Canal has recently been restored by the overseeing Trust, and hosted a gathering of narrow boats in April, 2012. Here on 8 April is an image in Droitwich of the restored Netherwich Basin with a number of working boats in attendance. Of the sixteen boats on show, at the front is 1926 FMC motor boat *Emu*, just behind is 1935 GUCC butty Star class *Canis Major*, then 1935 GUCC motor star class *Lacerta*, and 1935 GUCC motor Star class *Archimedes*. On the left is 1935 GUCC motor Star class *Aquarius* and 1926 FMC motor *Ibex* and 1934 icebreaker tug Stewarts & Lloyds *Bittell*.

On 25 June, 2010, a number of working boats went south on the Oxford Canal to visit the Braunston gathering. Here going through Hillmorton Lock number 7 is *Corona*, a Grand Union Canal Carrying Company motor boat Star class built by Harland & Wolff of Woolwich, London in 1935 with steel composite hull and fleet number 32.

At Hillmorton Lock number 2, Oxford Canal, on 25 June, 2010, going through together are *Cactus* and *Ling*. *Cactus* is a Fellows, Morton & Clayton motor boat built at Yarwoods of Woolwich in 1935 with iron composite hull, a Bolinder engine and fleet number 329. This boat in 2013 will have been with the same owner for 50 years. *Ling* is a Fellows, Morton & Clayton motor boat Fish class built by Yarwoods in 1934 with iron composite hull and fleet number 317.

Opposite: *Cactus* and *Ling* head towards Bridge 71 and Hillmorton Locks 4 and 5 on the Oxford Canal on 25 June, 2010. On the right of the picture just out of sight is Granthams Bridge over a short arm canal and a boatbuilders yard.

Below: On 25 June, 2010, at Hillmorton on the Oxford Canal, approaching Moors Bridge is working boat *Bletchley*, a Grand Union Canal Carrying Company motor boat Town class built by Harland & Wolff of Woolwich in 1936 with steel composite hull and fleet number 119. *Bletchley* is still a working boat and delivers fuel to the canalside dwellers.

On 25 June, 2010, at Hillmorton on the Oxford Canal, approaching Moors Bridge is working boat *Roach*, a Fellows, Morton & Clayton motor boat Fish class built by Yarwoods of Northwich in 1935 with iron composite hull and fleet number 322. She is still a working boat and is used to deliver fuel in the Midlands from the owner's coal yard at Bratch on the Staffordshire and Worcestershire Canal, and in the owner's livery.

On 25 June, 2010, at Hillmorton on the Oxford Canal, approaching Moors Bridge is *Darley* a Grand Union Canal Carrying Company motor boat Town class built by Harland & Wolff of Woolwich, London in 1937 of steel hull and fleet number 135.

An image of *Darley's* cabin in British Waterways livery as she sails under Moors Bridge.

On 10 April, 2012, at the newly-restored Droitwich Barge Canal in Netherwich Basin in Droitwich is a line-up of five working boats. The Droitwich Barge Canal is one of the oldest in the country, designed by eminent canal engineer James Brindley, which opened in 1771, primarily for the transportation of salt. The Droitwich Barge Canal is now open from the River Severn to the Netherwich Basin in Droitwich, a 21 mile ring including the short Droitwich Junction Canal of 1854, now also restored from Hanbury Wharf on the Worcester & Birmingham Canal to Netherwich Basin in Droitwich. It is recorded that the last boat to use the Droitwich Barge Canal was in 1918. The Junction Canal lasted a while longer, but the canals became derelict over the 50 years before the 1970s when the Droitwich Canal Trust was set up to restore the canal in its entirety. This came to fruition in 2011.

Opposite: The icebreaker tug *Laplander* is moored at Netherwich Basin in Droitwich on the Droitwich Barge Canal on 10 April, 2012. *Laplander* is steam driven, but originally from c.1830 a horse-drawn boat, later converted to diesel before steam was fitted by the current owner. She is a Birmingham Canal Navigation boat.

Locks are the most important feature on the canals: simply they are a device for transporting craft from one water level to another. There are some heavy gradients on a number of our canals, where a number of locks called flights are required to gain height. This is Hatton Flight. There are 21 locks at Hatton, the flight span being less than 2miles (3.2 kilometres) with a total rise of 148 feet (45 metres). Hatton Flight was opened in 1799 on the then Warwick and Birmingham Canal which became the Grand Union Canal in 1929. This image is looking up the locks from the Waterways Board offices, about two thirds of the way up, and towards Birmingham.

This image is from the same viewpoint but looking towards Warwick. The Hatton Flight became known as the "Stairway to Heaven" due to the difficulties in ascending, and then of course the easier passage to Birmingham and wages from then on. The locks were widened to 14 feet (4.3 metres) and a concrete lock system fitted to allow navigation by industrial boats of wider beam or two single narrow boats in tandem, in the mid 1930s.

At Hatton Flight is this preserved Piling Boat. This maintenance boat was first used in the 1950s, and designed with a shallow draft in order to allow access in tight or difficult positions on the canals. The boat was used to shore up canal banks using a piling rig mounted on the boat. There would also be a winch drum and small slave engine. Piles are stakes or cylinders driven into the ground to support or retain foundations or banks on the canal. Over the years the piles have been made of the following: wood, concrete, steel and currently coiled coir mats.

On 28 June, 2010, on the Grand Union Canal near Long Buckby, Northamptonshire, is narrow boat *Plover*, a Fellows, Morton & Clayton motor boat built at FMC Saltley works in Birmingham in 1915 of iron composite hull and fleet number 94.

On 28 June, 2010, on the Grand Union Canal near Long Buckby, Northamptonshire, is narrow boat *Owl* a Fellows, Morton & Clayton motor boat built by Yarwoods of Northwich in 1928 of iron composite hull and fleet number 211. The boat is now an undercloth conversion.

On 28 June, 2010, on the Grand Union Canal at Long Buckby, Northamptonshire, is narrow boat *Cyprus* an Erewash Canal Carrying Company motor boat built in 1935 of iron composite hull. This company was an autonomous subsidiary of the Grand Union Canal Carrying Company and had four boats named: *Ash* a butty; *Cedar* a butty; *Cyprus* a motor boat and *Elm* also a motor boat. *Cyprus* was teamed with *Cedar* and *Elm* with *Ash*. They were built 1 foot shorter than similar Star class boats to enable them to pass through the tight Zouch Lock on the Leicester Canal. The Erewash Canal is in Derbyshire, and runs from the River Trent to Cromford Basin, a distance of 12 miles and 14 locks.

Edstone Aqueduct at Bearley on the Stratford upon Avon Canal at 475 feet (145metres) is the longest aqueduct in England and crosses: a minor road; the North Warwickshire Railway; the Stratford upon Avon to Snow Hill Station, Birmingham line; and the former now long closed Alcester Railway. The Stratford upon Avon Canal was built between 1793 and 1816. Principal Engineer was William Clowes. At 25.5 miles (41km) long with 56 locks, it starts at Kings Norton and finishes at Stratford upon Avon Canal Basin where it joins the River Avon. The canal also connects to the Worcester & Birmingham Canal and the Grand Union Canal. The canal was closed in 1939 and restored in 1964. It is unusual in that the towpath is at the level of the canal bottom. Note the Transport Trust 'Red Wheel' award plaque on the right hand side in the image of the aqueduct above.

Unique to the Stratford upon Avon, or South Stratford, Canal, are these distinctive barrel-roofed lockkeepers' cottages. It is not known why they were built this way but one theory is that the canal craftsmen who built them were so used to constructing barrel-vaulted bridges that they used the same technique for the lock cottages roofs. Here are three examples, much modified, though the barrel shape can still be seen. They are the last three towards the Kingswood Junction where the Stratford upon Avon Canal meets the Grand Union Canal. Also shown is a typical heavy cast iron lozenge-shaped bridge warning sign erected by the Great Western Railway who controlled the canal at the time the signs were erected.

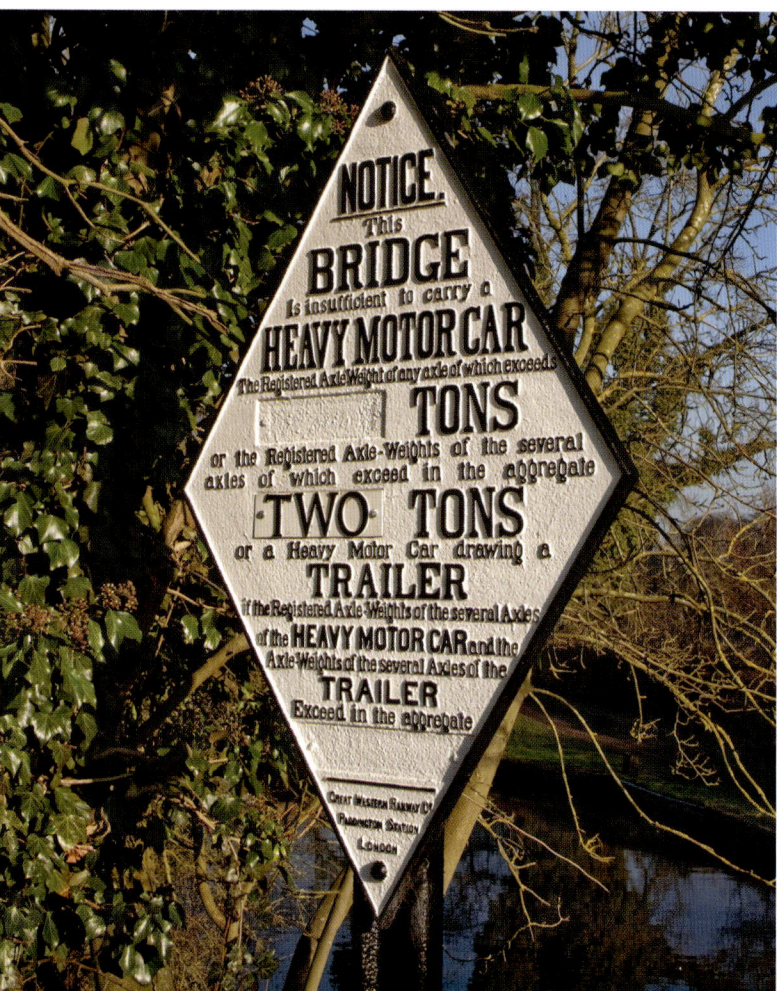